Four Attributes of Employee Engagement

And How To Develop Them

Thomas J. McCoy

DEDICATION

This book is dedicated to all of you who want to develop a company culture that calls forth engagement from your employees.

CONTENTS

Four Attributes of Employee Engagement

Chapter 1

TRUST

How To Develop An Environment Of Trust...

That Enables Your Employees To Succeed

The Purpose

The purpose of this Chapter is to:

1. Understand why trust is essential for an organization to accomplish its objectives.

2. Understand the two key conditions that must be present in order for trust to exist.

3. Learn how to initiate a process that will create an environment of trust.

The Benefit

This Chapter will enable you to:

1. Understand why employees lose trust.
2. Take action to fix the problem.

The Situation

Employees, working alone or in groups, are the only way an organization can accomplish its goals. The more efficient and effective employees are, the more success the organization will enjoy.

Employees are most efficient and effective when they are engaged in the business. That is, when they have a personal sense of focus, understanding, commitment, and accountability.

These four components of engagement are a function of personal desire. They exist in an individual in direct proportion to his or her desire to become involved and participate. When this desire is present, employees behave like business partners and provide an excellent return on investment.

Fear creates barriers to partnership and change. Fear acts to isolate an individual and shut down the desire to participate and become involved.

Without the desire to engage in the workplace, employees think, act and perform like hired hands. They consume more resources in terms of supervisory and administrative time and effort, and provide minimal contribution to the organization's success. They provide a poor return on investment.

> "Change is threatening to the fearful because it means that things may get worse." K. Whitney

The Foundation

Developing trust in the workplace is part of a structured effort to improve the way we work together and the results we obtain. Studies show that unless a safe social environment is present people will not open themselves up to partnership with others. They will not lower their emotional defenses and will not take the risk of allowing themselves to change.

Trust

Trust is reliance on the integrity, strength and ability of a person. Trust in an organization is the confidence that these same attributes are held by all employees and are an essential part of the implementation of all policies and administrative procedures.

In an environment of trust, people feel free and safe to express their thoughts. They come to understand that mistakes are not linked to punishment. Rather, mistakes are considered opportunities to learn that which they did not know. Growth becomes a goal, along with participation and contribution.

It's important not to confuse trust with mistakes. A mistake is an unintentional error. It is possible to trust a person who makes errors because trust is all about intent. (Trust, but verify.)

The Problem

Trust is based on opinion and feeling. It is a result of personal experience or good reason (the experience of others.) The problem is, once this opinion or feeling has been established, it is very difficult to change.

Trust is a matter of degree and most of us live somewhere

 between *"I trust ---- entirely"* and *"I don't trust ---- at all."* The degree of trust that one holds for a superior, co-worker, subordinate or organization is the direct result of past experiences.

In any company, the degree of trust, both individual and organizational, can be *established by the leader*. If the leader insists on the highest level of integrity then high integrity will be exhibited by all employees.

However, because we are human, we are not perfect. The faults in our behavior and our personal weaknesses provide the basis of experience from which others develop their degree of trust about us.

As a result, some level of mistrust, either of individuals or of the organization, exists within all companies. It may be stronger in one company than in another. It may be stronger on an individual level than on an organizational level, but it exists. This mistrust is a powerful source of organizational dysfunction and a subtle, yet significant, drain on overall performance.

Time for Introspection

 You will get the most value out of this Chapter if you take a few moments to internalize the information by answering the following questions.

Using a scale of 1 to 10, with 1 being "very low" and 10 being "extremely high", apply the rating to the following question.

❖ What overall level of trust exists within your company?

❖ Why did you give your company this rating? Be specific.

❖ Does this level have a significant effect on the performance of the organization? What would be the effect on the organization if the rating could be improved? Be specific.

The Solution

The solution to the problem of mistrust is found in the two attributes that create trust. These attributes are listed in the order in which they must occur.

1. Caring
2. Consistency

Understanding the attributes that create trust enables us to take action and change the negative effects of past actions.

Easy as 1, 2...

Establishing trust becomes an ongoing act. Regardless of what others do, you can develop a high level of personal trust by practicing these two attributes.

1. Caring: If I am concerned for your welfare and make a conscious effort to show my concern, what will your opinion or feeling be about me? If my intentions are positive and I take your best interests into consideration, will your opinion or feeling about me be favorable?

2. Consistency: And if I <u>always</u> exhibit the same caring behavior toward you, time after time, will you begin to accept that behavior as my true nature? Something you can rely on to occur? Will you begin to trust me?

It is a fact of human nature. When people are consistently treated in a caring manner, they develop trust. This applies to all people; employees, managers, customers, suppliers, spouses, children and everyone else.

Time for Introspection

You will get the most value out of this Chapter if you take a few moments to internalize the information by answering the following questions.

❖ How does the attribute of Caring show up in your behavior? The behavior of your co-workers? In your company? Be specific.

❖ What would the effect be if this were to increase? Be specific.

❖ How does the attribute of Consistency show up in your behavior? The behavior of your co-workers? In your company? Be specific.

❖ What would the effect be if this were to increase? Be specific.

Summary

Trust delivers a unique benefit to those who hold it and to the organizations that have it. It makes people receptive to support and encouragement. In this condition, people are more inclined to participate and become engaged in the group's objectives. They are open to dialogue and personal and professional development. They become more efficient and effective.

Want to improve the quality of your work experience and the organization's results? Practice consistent caring.

 **Time for Introspection**

You will get the most value out of this Chapter if you take a few moments to internalize the information by answering the following questions.

For You

❖ How do you plan to introduce the concepts of Caring and Consistency into your behavior? Be specific.

❖ What do you think the effect will be on your relationships? Why?

For Others and the Organization

❖ What can you do to introduce the concepts of Caring and Consistency to others in the organization? Who are they? Why would they benefit? Be specific.

❖ What do you think the effect will be on the organization? Why?

❖ **What rewards will employees receive for embracing this change? What's in it for them?**

Chapter 2

EMPOWERMENT

Five Steps That Develop A High Involvement, High Performance Workforce

The Purpose

The purpose of this Chapter is to:

1. Provide understanding about the concept of Empowerment
2. Present a model you can use to develop Empowerment in your company.

> *"As we help to raise our employees' self-esteem, we also increase their personal power. When we encourage them to be* confident, self-reliant, self-directed, and responsible individuals, we are giving them power." *Louise Hart*

The Benefit

This Chapter will enable you to:

1. Understand Empowerment
2. Encourage Empowerment
3. Benefit from Empowerment

The Situation

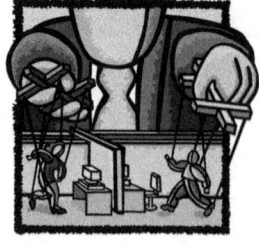

Empowerment is one of the most difficult and essential elements to developing a high-involvement, high-performance workforce. It is difficult because it requires allocating responsibility by releasing some portion of control to your employees. This is essential because it is a proven method for engaging your workforce in the business. By surrendering control to the employees you gain control over the business.

The Definition

A good definition of empowerment is *the authority and the ability to take independant action, within well defined parameters, which will actively influence the outcome.*

A group cannot be empowered. Empowerment takes place on an individual level. It is relative. Empowerment depends on the situation and the "ability" of the individual. A wise manager does not empower an employee until the employee has shown that he/she understands the effects of his/her actions on the success of the company and has demonstrated the ability to perform appropriately.

Get the Systems in Place

The process of empowering the workforce requires systems that provide information and which encourage understanding, learning and practice.

Time for Introspection

 You will get the most value out of this Chapter if you take a few moments to internalize the information by answering the following questions.

Empowerment requires information, understanding, learning and practice.

❖ On a scale of 1 to 10 with 1 being the lowest, how well do the majority of your employees understand the company's strategy? The business plan? Their role in helping achieve success?

❖ What information would improve your employees "line-of-sight" to the company's goals? Be specific in your list.

A Five Step Strategy for Empowerment

Empowerment requires an implementation strategy. The following 5 steps have proven successful in creating a culture of empowered employees, focused on improving the value of the business.

1. Clearly Define the Outcome

In terms of Empowerment, clearly define what the organization wants, and why.

• What: "We want employees to have the ability (skills and expertise) and authority (permission) to make decisions and take action within clearly defined job parameters with the intention of achieving the company's objectives and to understand & accept responsibility for the outcomes of those decisions and actions."

- Why: The purpose of empowering the workforce is to enable it to better fulfill the mission of your company. *Insert your mission statement here.*

Time for Introspection

Take a moment to answer the following questions:

❖ Why do you want empowered employees? How important is it to you? What value will it bring? Be specific

❖ What type of empowerment do you want for your company? Be specific.

❖ Do you have a mission statement? If not, you must develop one.

2. Provide Management with the Skills

It is essential to help all levels of management develop the ability to allocate responsibility and release control. This requires education, training and may require individual coaching.

Time for Introspection

Take a moment to answer the following questions:

❖ Which managers in your company will support empowerment?

❖ Which managers will resist it?

❖ How will you overcome resistance? How will you show your support for the empowerment process? Make a list and be specific.

3. Develop Your Employees

Empowerment, on an individual level, is accepting responsibility and acting accordingly. To develop an empowered workforce it is necessary to grow people's capacity to assume more responsibility. This requires education and training that develops key skills.

Some key skills and the training necessary to develop them are provided in the following list.

- Critical thinking skills
  - Goal Setting
  - Problem Solving
  - Decision Making
  - Risk Analysis

- Performance analysis & feedback skills
  - Real-time data collected locally
  - Analyzed locally
  - Real-time data acted upon locally
    1) Action Planning Skills

- Coaching Skills
  - Relationship skills

- Influencing Skills
  People are empowered if they have the capacity to be a compelling force on the actions of others for the

betterment of the organization. Some tactics that will help your employees develop the capacity to produce effects on the outcome by influencing others are as follows.

- Understand the line-of-sight of other individuals or groups
    1) Conduct cross-function ScoreCard alignment discussions.
- Group dialogue to understand the shared destiny. Connect career, professional or financial aspirations with the aspirations of the organization.
    1) Incentive pay system
    2) Performance evaluation system
    3) Personal development plans
        (a) Develop a knowledge, skills and abilities matrix
    4) Merit increase system
    5) Develop career paths promotion levels and growth opportunities

Time for Introspection

Take a moment to answer the following questions:

❖ From the information you just read, make a list of tactics that currently exist for the:

- Leadership group
- Middle managers
- Front line managers and supervisor
- General workforce

❖ Now make a list of the tactics that need to be developed for each group.

❖ How do you plan do develop these tactics? Be specific and prioritize the list.

4. Develop a Common Understanding

Empowerment is only effective when everyone has a common understanding of the concept, the performance objectives and their part in the effort. Empowerment relies on a well defined set of Values that are subscribed to by all.

Beliefs and values create a sense of identity and clear expectations. They become the moral criteria by which decisions are made and prioritized. It is essential that the members of the group hold similar values. To nurture the proper values, we must develop a common mind-set around shared responsibility.

- Empowerment requires the personal value of Self-Responsibility! It requires self-choice; the belief that one can change if one chooses to change. It requires one to accept responsibility for one's actions, feelings and beliefs and understand that they are the foundation of one's behavior. It requires the desire and ability to determine and direct one's actions and thoughts.
  - Tactic: Conduct an *Understanding Our Values* workshop to encourage and develop understanding, personal acceptance and commitment.

Develop and communicate a unifying explanation of what your business is about. This "purpose" gives everyone direction and a way to evaluate the quality of their decisions.

- Help employees develop line-of-sight to the purpose, vision, mission, values and incentive ScoreCard objectives as the basis of decision making.
  - Tactic: Conduct an *Understanding Our Mission* workshop. Mission-based decision making develops a common focus on mutually serving a clearly identified purpose.
  - Tactic: Conduct an *Understanding Our Customer* workshop that develops an understanding of and relationship to your customers' needs and expectations.

Reality Check: Not every employee will respond well to empowerment. Be prepared to address this issue.

- Accomplishments are a foundation of empowerment. As such it is important to recognize progress and identify role models. We can begin to empower the workforce through activities such as:
  - Identify and celebrate Role Models. Develop a method for employees to see and share success stories/examples
  - Celebrate accomplishments
  - Document examples of empowerment
  - Develop recognition programs and demonstrations of appreciation for contribution.

Time for Introspection

Take a moment to answer the following questions:

❖ What values does your company currently support? Do your employees understand them? How are they emphasized in the workplace?

❖ What values should be added?

❖ Does your company have a unifying focus? What is the vision of what you want the company to be? Do the employees understand it? How do you know?

❖ What do you currently do to show recognition for participation and contribution?

❖ What could you do?

5. Establish Accountability

Empowerment without accountability is a recipe for chaos. Accountability is that aspect of responsibility where results and outcomes are discussed. Accountability is a form of trust and trusting people empowers them.

There are several proven tactics that can be used to develop accountability.

- Define and clearly communicate expectations for all roles.
  - Examples are: the purpose of the role, the customers served by that role (internal and external), the deliverables provided to those customers. This list is often developed during the design stage when developing an incentive ScoreCard™.
  - These expectations and role descriptions should be incorporated into Individual position descriptions.

- Develop and communicate department statements
    - Develop statements of purpose, of mission, and of service level agreements for each department.

- Responsibility charting
    - Identify a list of responsibilities for each role within the department as it applies to the department and company mission statements.
    - Create *Action Plans* to increase individual responsibility

- Authority matrix: a robust Empowerment tool
    - Define the decision-making authority for each position.
        1) Authority over what? When? Under what circumstances?
    - Develop criteria for expanding this authority.
    - Build skills and experience to expand the authority
    - Approve the authority and expand the matrix.

- Develop processes that enables employees to practice and apply their empowerment.
    - Participate in important decisions
    - Cross-functional interaction and influence
    - Self-directed work teams

Time for Introspection

Take a moment to answer these questions:

❖   Do your employees clearly understand what is expected of them? How do you know?

❖ How do you measure performance on a company, department, team and individual level? Be specific

❖ Do you have a list of Value Drivers for your company? What are they?

❖ How often do you discuss the performance of these value drivers with your employees? Should it be more frequently?

Summary

Empowerment is an essential part of a culture of partnership where each employee thinks and acts like a business partner.

In this workplace culture you invite employees to participate in a high-involvement, high-performance environment. In order to engage them it is essential to provide the appropriate rewards.

Take a moment to answer the following question:

❖ **What rewards will employees receive for embracing this change to Empowerment? What's in it for them?**

Chapter 3

Teamwork

How To Identify the Four Dysfunctions of a Team...

And Resolve Them

The Purpose

The purpose of this Chapter is to:

1. Provide an understanding of the four aspects of human behavior that undermine the team process

2. Develop insight as to what actions can be taken to repair the damage and return to a normal functioning team.

The Benefit

This Chapter will enable you to:

1. Understand why teams become dysfunctional and

2. How to fix the problem.

The Situation

A team is nothing more than a group of people acting together in a coordinated effort.

The fundamental reason teams have value is because they access the power of multiple perspectives; multiple ways of understanding and knowing about an issue or topic.

This team power is normally used to solve problems or develop new ideas, and the outcome is often focused on the accomplishment of a project. Occasionally, as with self-directed work groups, the team concept is used to encourage the

flexible application of labor and skills i.e. "help wherever you can to accomplish the job."

The Foundation

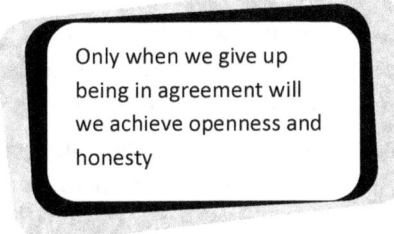

Only when we give up being in agreement will we achieve openness and honesty

Teamwork is a structured effort to improve the way we work together. There are several models for developing and maintaining teams. However, the foundation of a successful team is based on authentic communication.

In an environment where people feel free and safe to express their thoughts, they will be able to learn, grow and help others. Unfortunately, all too often, the team develops a mistaken sense that all members must be in agreement. Agreement eliminates conflict. However, it also eliminates individuality, and individuality is the heart and soul of the power of the team. So only when the team gives up being in agreement will it be able to achieve openness and honesty.

Exchange of Ideas and Opinions

Openness and honesty is the result of dialogue. It's the result of gathering and analyzing divergent points of view from individual members in order to build a shared

understanding and create something NEW. A successful dialogue requires that all members are willing to be influenced by others, that they are willing to adjust their actions, behaviors or opinions based on the views and opinions of others.

The difference between discussion and dialogue is that discussion involves advocating your point of view and dialogue requires that you listen unconditionally, with no agenda or filters. Listening is a combination of hearing and interpretation. Interpretation is the "truth" we develop for ourselves based on our background, our beliefs and our values.

Since these are individual traits, each person develops their own individual "truth." By listening with no agenda or filters we are able to hear what the other person is saying. Using unbiased listening, conversation ("This is what that means to me.") and inquiry ("What does that mean to you?") we can establish a common meaning and arrive at understanding as to the interpretation. This understanding becomes the binding force of the team.

Time for Introspection

 You will get the most value out of this Chapter if you take a few moments to internalize the information by answering the following questions:

❖ Are you willing to be influenced by others? Why? Why not?

❖ What must you do to allow yourself to be influenced by others? Be specific. What form does that take? What does that look like?

❖ What process or tactic could you use to encourage team members to allow themselves to be influenced by others on their team?

The Problem

The problem with teams is they are composed of people. And the problem with people is they are subject to the four fundamental aspects of being human. These four fundamental aspects are:

1. The need to be right
2. The need to win
3. The need to justify actions or behaviors
4. The need to dominate

These four aspects are the source of all dysfunction within a team.

The success of a team depends on each member's willingness to align with rather than agree with the team's goals, strategies and tactics.

To align with something that you may not necessarily agree with requires humility, compassion and commitment. The four aspects of being human are contrary to humility, compassion and commitment and they invariably cause conflict and undermine the team.

Time for Introspection

 You will get the most value out of this Chapter if you take a few moments to internalize the information by answering the following questions:

When one person needs to be Right, another person has to be wrong.

❖ How does the need to be Right show up in your behavior? List examples.

❖ How does the need to be Right show up in the behavior of team members? What is the effect on the team's performance?

❖ What would be the effect on the team if all members gave up their need to be Right? Be specific.

When one person needs to Win, another person has to lose.

❖ How does the need to Win show up in your behavior? List examples.

❖ How could the need to Win show up in the behavior of team members? What is the effect on the team's performance?

❖ What would be the effect on the team if all members gave up their need to win? Be specific.

When we Justify, we provide a "satisfactory" reason or excuse that allows us to declare ourselves innocent or blameless. We do this to protect our ego. However, the problem with justification is that it compromises our integrity.

Integrity is based on honoring our word, on doing what we say we will do. When we justify not doing what we said or implied we would do ("Sorry I'm late to the meeting but...") we damage our integrity with ourselves and with our team members.

Integrity is a fundamental aspect of trust. When integrity is compromised, trust is compromised and the group can no longer work as a team because the members cannot be relied upon.

❖ How does the need to Justify show up in your behavior? List examples.

❖ How does the need to Justify show up in the behavior of team members? What is the effect on the team's performance? Be specific.

❖ What would the effect be if every member accepted ownership of the consequences of their behavior and did not attempt to Justify their actions?

When one person Dominates, another person is controlled.

❖ How does the need to Dominate show up in your behavior? List examples.

❖ How could the need to Dominate show up in the behavior of team members? What is the effect on the team's performance?

❖ What would the effect be if every team member gave up their need to Dominate?

The Solution

The solution to the problem of the four dysfunctions of a team starts with understanding the cause of the problems. The cause is that people make relationship mistakes because they are human and are influenced by the four aspects of being human:

1. The need to be right
2. The need to win
3. The need to justify
4. The need to dominate

Understanding the causes of relationship mistakes enables us to dissolve the effects of these mistakes. We can dissolve the effects through a willingness to forgive. It's as simple, and as hard, as that!

People make mistakes. If they are mistakes, and not intentional harms, then forgiveness is the answer to making things whole again.

Easy as 1, 2, 3

So, forgiveness becomes an ongoing act. When (not if) I make a relationship mistake it is due to the fact I was driven by the need to be right, or win, or justify, or dominate and I can correct it.

1. Because I understand the cause, I can forgive myself (I'm not bad, I'm human.)

28

2. Because it was a mistake, I can resolve to do better, realizing that I am striving for progress, not perfection.
3. Because I want to make amends, I can apologize and ask forgiveness from my team members.

When a team member makes a relationship mistake, because the team understands the cause, the team can have a dialogue about the mistake, seek a commitment to improve, forgive the mistake, and move forward as a team.

When management makes a relationship mistake (yep, they're human too,) if the team understands the cause, the affected group can have a dialogue about the mistake, seek a commitment to improve, forgive the mistake, and move forward in the relationship.

Summary

How do we resolve the Four Dysfunctions of a team and keep the team functioning?

1. Understand the four human causes
2. Maintain an ongoing willingness to give and accept forgiveness.

Time for Introspection

 You will get the most value out of this Chapter if you take a few moments to internalize the information by answering the following questions.

The Four fundamental elements of being human

❖ How do you plan to introduce these concepts into the team environment? Be specific.

❖ What do you think will be the effect on the team? Why?

Forgiveness

❖ How do you plan to introduce the concept of forgiveness into the team environment? Be specific.

❖ What do you think will be the effect on the team? Why?

❖ What tactical process can the team use to address relationship mistakes and provide forgiveness?

❖ **What rewards will employees receive for embracing this change? What's in it for them?**

Chapter 4

Innovation

How To Build Practical Innovation Into Your Company

Four Steps To Thinking Outside The Box

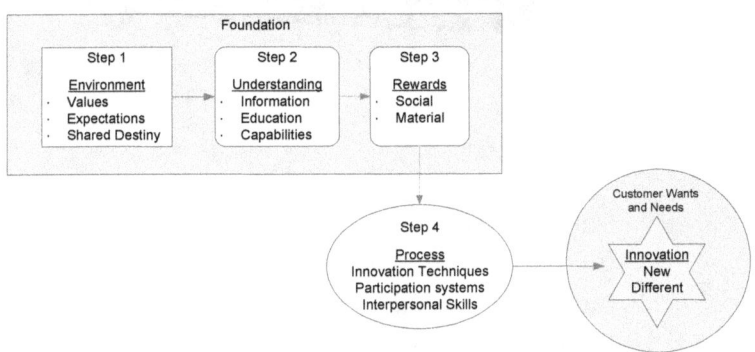

The Purpose

The purpose of this Chapter is to:

1. Provide understanding about the concept of Innovation

2. Present a model you can use to develop innovation in your company.

> "The problem is never how to get new, innovative thoughts into your mind, but how to get old ones out. Every mind is a building filled with archaic furniture. Clean out a corner of your mind and creativity will instantly fill it." *Dee Hock*

The Benefit

This Chapter will enable you to:

1. Understand innovation
2. Encourage innovation
3. Benefit from innovation

The Situation

Survival in today's marketplace requires more than access to capital, technology and low cost labor. These are no longer competitive advantages.

 Marketplace dynamics such as the internet, social media, rapid prototyping and global outsourcing have established a "niche market" business environment where "niche markets" flourish and which requires rapid response.

Business opportunities exist only for a short period before they are captured. Companies become dominant by offering fulfillment for needs and wants that customers were unaware they had. Nimble companies thrive in this environment and business-as-usual companies suffer or perish. The difference between the two is...innovation.

Minnesota-based Tennant Co. recently observed its 135th anniversary. The CEO of this manufacturing company with 2,500 employees attributes survival to "its ability to nimbly change with the times and create innovative products." Tennant started as a lumber company and now produces industrial floor-maintenance equipment, street sweepers and carpet cleaners.

Who? New? or Different?

Innovation means bringing something new into an area, to create something that did not exist before.

In a business setting this creativity is based on actions performed by employees. Therefore, it is important to identify whom we want to be innovative and define what actions we want them to take. Do we want all employees to be innovative?

Do we want them to identify and develop new products? Or do we want them to identify and develop different ways of conducting our current business?

Most companies don't want to become design studios. Most companies want their employees to become more engaged in the business, to contribute more of their mental capabilities to helping the company grow and prosper.

These companies are looking for wide-spread, practical innovation. The kind where the workforce will identify and implement new or different ways of conducting current business.

Steps 1, 2, and 3: The Foundation

This form of practical innovation requires a solid foundation on which to build. Establishing this foundation involves three of the four steps to thinking outside the box. These three are: Environment, Understanding and Rewards.

1. The Environment

Innovation requires a safe, nurturing environment of trust in which to take hold and flourish. Such an environment should encourage calculated risk taking and should view failure as a learning experience. Perfection is not considered a value and punishment is not part of the trial-error-correction-trial learning cycle.

This environment is often defined as a partnering environment. It includes values that encourage innovation, statements that clearly defined expectations about innovation, empowerment that permits innovation and a sense of shared destiny that encourages partnering with others.

2. Understanding

Understanding is the heart of the creative experience. It is the ability to grasp and explain the meaning of something. Understanding works on a subliminal level, allowing the sub-conscious mind to identify unseen patterns and resolve problems. The outcome of this process is called intuition.

Intuition is to know something without having to discover, perceive or prove it. Research shows that this mode of thinking is an essential part of the innovative thought process. So, understanding is the raw material of intuition!

If an organization wants to nurture innovation it will need to accept and support an approach to reasoning that is not solely supported by empirical logic. The more we understand a topic, project or problem, the better equipped we are to engage our sub-conscious mind, our intuition, to come up with innovative thoughts about the topic.

For many organizations, this is an insurmountable obstacle. They are hide-bound in their need to be "protected" by the data. They act as if data is the only source of understanding.

To gain understanding we need focus, information and education.

- ❖ Focus is necessary to direct our thinking toward a particular topic, the better to produce useful results.
- ❖ Information provides us with facts and data about the topic on which we are focused.
- ❖ Education helps us develop an awareness of the relationships between the facts and data. These relationships and patterns impart meaning to the data. The deeper our understanding of the meaning, the more raw material our intuition has to work with.

What information do we need? Well, the assumption is that we want to become more innovative in order to better fulfill the needs of our customers. Therefore, when starting the innovative process, it is essential to understand as much as possible about our current capabilities, our customers' needs, and their customers' needs.

3. Rewards

The act of innovation requires taking a social risk. It requires thought and action that is outside the norm. For most of us, the workplace is our primary source of income. As such, we assume a cautious attitude about our behavior at work, so as not to jeopardize our source of financial security.

This conservative attitude stifles creative thinking. To change it is necessary to provide strong reasons for employees to think and act in new patterns and to participate in the innovative process.

Two of the strongest reasons for change are pay and position. Linking pay, perhaps in the form of incentive, to the outcome of an innovative effort is a strong way to encourage participation. Providing social recognition and elevated status to those who participate in innovative efforts sends the message that innovation is a good thing.

Time for Introspection

 You will get the most value out of this Chapter if you take a few moments to internalize the information by answering the following questions.

An innovative environment requires certain values, expectations, empowerment and sense of shared destiny.

❖ What examples of these components currently exist in your organization? Be specific. What form do they take?

❖ What examples of these components should exist in order to develop and support an environment of innovation? Be specific.

❖ What needs to be done to include these components in your organization? Who needs to develop them? Who needs to approve them? How will they be established in the culture?

Understanding is the raw material of intuition.

❖ How does your company treat intuition? Be specific.

❖ If your company wants to nurture innovation, what needs to be done? Be specific.

The end result we want to achieve from our effort to be a more innovative company is to better serve the customer.

❖ How does your company obtain the Voice-Of-The Customer?

❖ Who in your company understands the customers' needs and wants? The needs and wants of your customers' customer?

❖ Who should have this understanding?

❖ What can be done to improve access to the voice-of-the-customer; the facts, data and information about customer needs and wants? Be specific.

❖ What social and material rewards does your organization use to encourage intuitive thinking and innovative action?

❖ What social and material rewards should it use? Be specific?

Step 4: The Process

The fourth step to creating a workplace where employees think outside the box is to establish a Process for Innovation. This process should enable employees to develop new or different responses to customer needs & wants and timely responses to competitive issues.

The process for innovation includes participation systems, interpersonal skills, innovation techniques and a review process.

A. Participation systems are an established process through which employees can become engaged in the effort. Most participation systems are team oriented. This takes advantage of group dynamics to expand understanding and intuitive thinking. The type of participation system depends on the innovation objective. If the objective is to develop a new product or service, then a project team would work well. If the objective is to do current activities differently, then a group system centered on the department would work well.

B. Interpersonal skills act as a social lubricant that improves performance and results. They are necessary to enhance the effectiveness of the group and to avoid the 4 dysfunctions of a team.

C. Innovation techniques are specific techniques designed to get people thinking outside the box. These range from creative "warm up" games to Action Planning sessions and team suggestion projects. Defining terms, reframing concepts, and questioning assumptions, ideas, patterns, rules & relationships are fundamental, easy-to-use techniques that create deeper understanding and stimulate intuition.

D. The outcome of the team's innovative efforts should be reviewed on a timely and ongoing basis. This external review provides valuable perspective which contributes to the team's insight.

Rarely does the end result of innovation spring forth full blown. More often it is a process of steps, where each step builds on the previous step until heretofore unknown relationships and patterns become apparent.

Time for Introspection

 You will get the most value out of this Chapter if you take a few moments to internalize the information by answering the following questions:

❖ What types of participation systems exist in your company?

❖ What types of participation systems should be established as a forum for innovative thinking?

❖ What interpersonal skills does an innovation team need? Why do they need these skills? What will be the benefit of having these skills? Be specific.

❖ What techniques are currently used in group settings to provide direction to the innovative process? What missing techniques could be added? What value would they bring to the process?

The Summary

The 4 step model represents a methodology for creating a work culture which encourages engagement and supports innovative thinking.

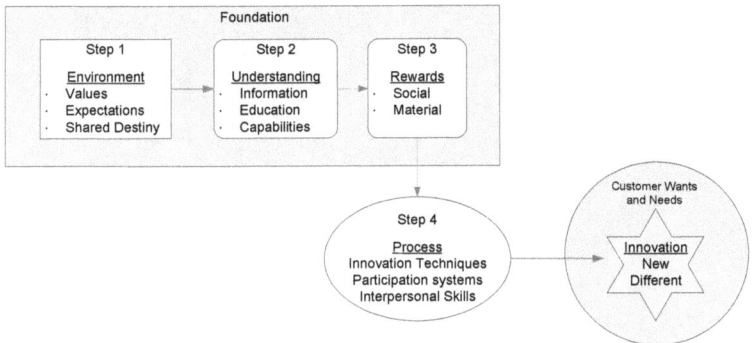

We can use this methodology to identify the unarticulated needs and wants of our customers, and their customers, and design solutions that place us ahead of the competition.

Innovation isn't about technology, or trends, or even the competition, it's about engaging the workforce and understanding and serving the customer.

Time for Introspection

❖ What efforts exist in your company to identify unarticulated customer needs and wants?

❖ What efforts should exist? Be specific.

❖ Who should participate in these efforts? Why? Be specific.

❖ **What rewards will employees receive for embracing this change to Innovation? What's in it for them?**

Four Attributes of Employee Engagement

Additional Books by Thomas McCoy on the topic of Employee Engagement.

- *Employee Engagement: The Framework for the Future.* A guide for implementing an employee engagement system...and achieving a sustainable competitive advantage.

- *Employee Engagement Toolbox.* An indispensable set of tools that each employee needs to become engaged.

- *Creating an "Open-Book" Organization*...Where employees think and act like business partners.

- *Compensation and Motivation*: Maximizing employee performance with behavior-based incentive plans.

All books are available on Amazon and through the Employee Engagement Institute.
www.EmployeeEngagementInstitute.com

Get the Answers You Want!

Got a problem or observation that you would like to see included in the "Attributes of Employee Engagement" series?

Send it to:
tjmccoy@EmployeeEngagementInstitute.com Put: "Attention Attributes" in the subject line.

Get the Performance and Profit You Want!

Contact us today for a conversation on how to increase profit, grow your customer base, improve ease of operation and enhance your company value by engaging your employees to think and act like business partners.

Learn how to include Employee Engagement as a line item in the business strategy.

Thomas McCoy - Director
Employee Engagement Institute
tjmccoy@EmployeeEngagementInstitute.com
www.EmployeeEngagementInstitute.com
816-333-1261

ABOUT THE AUTHOR

Thomas McCoy is the Director of The Employee Engagement Institute. He has over 30 years experience in driving growth by engaging employees to think and act like business partners.

He is the author of four other books on the topic of company culture, employee engagement and performance improvement:

- *Employee Engagement: The Framework for the Future*, a guide for implementing a proven employee engagement system.
- *The Employee Engagement Toolbox*, a must-have manual for every employee.
- *Compensation and Motivation* (a textbook at Florida State)
- *Creating An Open-Book Organization* (nominated for SHRM book-of-the-year)

He has been quoted in Newsweek, featured in the Wall Street Journal and nominated for SHRM's Michael J. Losey research award for his forward looking work in the field of Human Resources. He designed and taught a *High Performance Workplace* seminar at George Washington University and is a frequent conference speaker.

He holds a Lean Six Sigma Certification from Villanova University, a Coaching by Design Certification from the Johnston Institute and a Bachelors of Fine Arts Degree from the University of Minnesota. He is a member of the Board of Directors for the Executive Service Corps of Greater Kansas City.